MW01131002

JAZZ PIANO COMPING

HARMONIES, VOICINGS, AND GROOVES

SUZANNE DAVIS

Edited by Jonathan Feist

This book is dedicated to my teachers Charlie Banacos
and Hal Crook, who changed the way I think about music.

Berklee Press

Vice President: David Kusek
Dean of Continuing Education: Debbie Cavalier
Assistant Vice President of Berklee Media/CFO: Robert F. Green
Managing Editor: Jonathan Feist
Editorial Assistants: Jimmy Haas, David Hume, Andrea Penzel, Jacqueline Sim, Won (Sara) Hwang
Cover Designer: Kathy Kikkert

ISBN 978-0-87639-125-9

1140 Boylston Street
Boston, MA 02215-3693 USA
(617) 747-2146

Visit Berklee Press Online at
www.berkleepress.com

DISTRIBUTED BY

HAL•LEONARD®
7777 W. BLUEMOUND RD. P.O. BOX 13819
MILWAUKEE, WISCONSIN 53213

Visit Hal Leonard Online at
www.halleonard.com

CONTENTS

AUDIO TRACKS

Tracks	Figure	Title
Track 1	1.1	Triads in Root Position and Inversions
Track 2	1.2	The Triad Experience
Track 3	1.2	The Triad Experience (No Keyboard)
Track 4	2.1	Seventh Chords in Root Position and Inversions
Track 5	2.2	Close and Open Voicings
Track 6	3.1	Smooth Voice Leading
Track 7	3.2	Common Tones and Stepwise Motion
Track 8	3.3	Low Voicing
Track 9	3.4	Voice Leading Alternative (Higher)
Track 10	3.5	Voice Leading with Melody
Track 11	4.1	II V I Expanded Shells with Two Hands
Track 12	4.2	Expanded Shells and Open Voicings
Track 13	4.2	Expanded Shells and Open Voicings (No Keyboard)
Track 14	5.1	Allowable Tensions
Track 15	5.2	How Tensions Resolve
Track 16	6.1	Comping with Guide Tones
Track 17	6.2	Guide Tones Plus One Tension
Track 18	6.3	Guide Tones Plus One Tension (LH) and Root (RH)
Track 19	7.1	Rootless Voicings with T9 and T13, "A" Position II V I Formula
Track 20	7.2	Rootless Voicings with T9 and T13, "B" Position II V I Formula
Track 21	7.3	"A" and "B" Position Voicings with Two Hands, with Root in LH
Track 22	7.4	II V I Rootless with 9 and 13, LH
Track 23	7.5	9, 13 LH Rootless with 5 and T9 in RH
Track 24	7.6	LH Plays 9, 13 Rootless Voicings; RH Plays 5, 9, 13
Track 25	8.1	Fourths Voicings in C Dorian
Track 26	8.2	Fourths Voicings for Two Hands
Track 27	9.1	Upper-Structure Triads and Fourths
Track 28	10.1	Open Voicings
Track 29	10.2	Open-Position Voicings with Tensions (Chord Progression)
Track 30	10.2	Open-Position Voicings with Tensions (Chord Progression, No Keyboard)

Tracks	Figure	Title
Track 31	10.4	"Blue in Purple"
Track 32	10.4	"Blue in Purple" (No Keyboard)
Track 33	12.1	Labeling the Chords with Chord Tones and Tensions
Track 34	12.2	Chord Progression 1: II V I, Two Hands
Track 35	12.3	Chord Progression 2: Jazz Blues, Two Hands
Track 36	12.3	Chord Progression 2: Jazz Blues, Two Hands (No Keyboard)
Track 37	13.5	"Blues for Mr. H.C."
Track 38	13.5	"Blues for Mr. H.C." (No Keyboard)
Track 39	14.2	Standard Rock (Even Eighths) Groove
Track 40	14.2	Standard Rock (Even Eighths) Groove (No Keyboard)
Track 41	14.3	Bossa Nova Groove
Track 42	14.3	Bossa Nova Groove (No Keyboard)
Track 43	14.4	Swing Groove
Track 44	14.4	Swing Groove (No Keyboard)
Track 45	14.5	Standard Rock 6/8 Groove
Track 46	14.5	Standard Rock 6/8 Groove (No Keyboard)
Track 47	14.6	Jazz Waltz Groove
Track 48	14.6	Jazz Waltz Groove (No Keyboard)
Track 49	14.7	"Groove Tune"
Track 50	14.7	"Groove Tune" (No Keyboard)
Track 51	14.8	"Jazz Ballad" Comping Using Textures, Arpeggiation, Fragmentation, and Block Chords
Track 52	15.1	Guitar and Piano Taking Turns Comping for Bass Solo (Rhythm Changes)
Track 53	16.1	Comping with LH while Playing Line in RH
Track 54	16.2	Comping with LH and Dropping Out LH to Solo with RH
Track 55	17.1	Soloist Plays Downbeats
Track 56	17.2	Soloist Plays Long Phrases
Track 57	17.3	Soloist Plays Short Phrases
Track 58	18.1	"The Dragonfly" (Comping with Rhythm Hits)
Track 59	18.1	"The Dragonfly" (No Keyboard)
Track 60	19.1	"The Standard Standard"
Track 61	19.1	"The Standard Standard" (No Keyboard)
Track 62	20.1	12-Bar Blues 1 (12/8 Feel R&B)
Track 63	20.1	12-Bar Blues 1 (12/8 Feel R&B, No Keyboard)
Track 64	20.2	12-Bar Blues 2 (New Orleans Style)
Track 65	20.2	12-Bar Blues 2 (New Orleans Style, No Keyboard)
Track 66	20.4	12-Bar Jazz Blues
Track 67	20.4	12-Bar Jazz Blues (No Keyboard)
Track 68	22.1	B♭ Rhythm Changes
Track 69	22.1	B♭ Rhythm Changes (No Keyboard)

INTRODUCTION

The term "comp" derives from the word "accompany." It refers to chording in general, but also, specifically, to the pianist's role as part of the rhythm section. Comping should provide support to and enhance a melody line. For this reason, the use of rhythm, syncopation, and space are very important concepts in comping.

Comping can also be defined as playing chords in the left hand to back up your own solo in the right hand. A soloist who is not a keyboard player may also be backed up by a keyboard player comping with one or both hands, either with a rhythm section (bass and drums) or without. Comping must always be considered in its rhythmic context. If there is no rhythm section, the solo keyboard player must provide the rhythmic feel of the piece. If playing with a bass and drums, the keyboard player becomes part of the overall groove.

You may have some experience comping either solo or in a group. Your keyboard playing experience might consist of some classical piano instruction, or perhaps you are self-taught. You may have some chord theory knowledge: you can play some types of seventh chords in root position and inversions. Some students can only play chords this way, only using the left hand, with a dependency on roots and root position in playing chords. This is not bad; it is simply being in beginner mode.

For this book to be useful to you, it is crucial to be able to spell and play on the keyboard, all triads and seventh chords, in all twelve keys, in all their inversions. If you can't do this now, you will be able to do so by the first two lessons.

Proceed slowly and methodically through the book, and only continue to the next lesson when you have mastered the one before it.

In comping, memorization is the key to learning. In teaching my students to comp, I do not allow them to write notes on a staff on a lead sheet (or names of notes) because memorization is so important.

It is vital for the jazz keyboard player to be able to interpret chord symbols for both triads and seventh chords with tensions. Tensions are the notes in the upper extension of a seventh chord (and can also be used with triads). This means that you must have a memorized repertoire of different voicings (specific arrangements of chords with or without tensions) for chords in all twelve keys, which you can use immediately without thinking. This is the goal; it obviously does not happen overnight. But memorizing as many voicings as possible is a major part of your commitment to learning how to comp. The more you do it, the easier it becomes. Enjoy your journey!

Triads

The most basic chords are triads. Many rock and pop tunes are composed solely using triads. The common chord symbols for triads in sheet music and lead sheets look like this:

Triad Chord Symbols

Symbol	Name	In root position
C	C major triad	R 3 5
C–	C minor triad	R ♭3 5
C+	C augmented triad	R 3 +5
C°	C diminished triad	R ♭3 dim5
Csus4	C suspended 4 triad	R sus4 5

Triads have three voicing positions: root position, first inversion, and second inversion. Listen to the triads on track 1, then play them.

TRACK 1

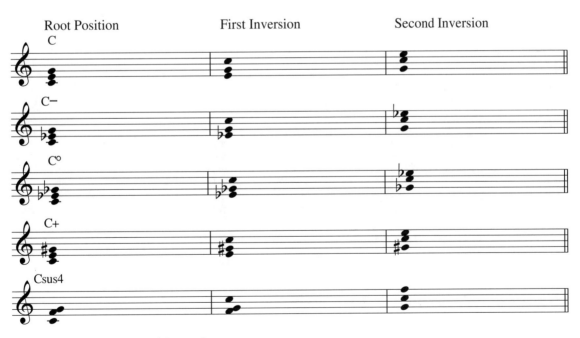

Fig. 1.1. Triads in Root Position and Inversions

Triads are most effective when played in the right hand, with the left hand playing the bass note in octaves. We will practice this in the following exercise.

Practice 1.1. The Triad Experience

TRACK 2   TRACK 3

Play along with the rhythm section on track 2, and when you're ready, play it on track 3, where there is no recorded keyboard. Fill in the triads indicated in figure 1.2 (writing them on the staff if you need to).

Fig. 1.2. The Triad Experience. Fill in the triads.

Practice 1.2. Memorizing Triads

Memorize the five types of triads (major, minor, diminished, augmented, and suspended) in all twelve keys, and practice them in their inversions before beginning the study of seventh chords (lesson 2), even though most jazz pieces use more seventh chords than triads. Sometimes, both types of chords are used, and you need to know how to cycle back and forth quickly.

LESSON 2

Seventh Chords: Required Seventh Chords in All Keys

A seventh chord is a triad with a 7 added. The triad can be major, minor, suspended, augmented, or diminished, and the 7 can be major, minor, or diminished.

Here are the common symbols for seventh chords. In bold are the ones used at Berklee College of Music and in this book.

There are nine types of seventh chords,

Chord	Notes	Common Symbol
1. Major 7	R 3 5 7	**Maj7**, Δ7
2. Dominant 7	R 3 5 ♭7	**7**
3. Dominant 7 sus4	R 4 5 7	**7sus4** or 7(sus4)
4. Minor 7	R ♭3 5 ♭7	**−7**, m7
5. Minor 7♭5*	R ♭3 ♭5 ♭7	**−7♭5** or m7♭5
6. Diminished 7	R ♭3 ♭5 °7	**°7** or dim7
7. Minor (Major 7)	R ♭3 5 7	**−Maj7** or m(Maj7)
8. Augmented Major 7	R 3 ♯5 7	**+Maj7**
9. Augmented 7	R 3 ♯5 ♭7	**+7** or aug7

*Minor 7♭5 is known in traditional harmony as "half diminished 7."

You must be fluent with these chords before you can learn more advanced voicings with tension substitutions.

- Be aware of the difference between "+Maj7" and "+7."

- Be sure you know your inversions.

ROOTS AND INVERSIONS

A seventh chord has four different voicing positions: root position and first, second, and third inversions. Here are some examples of inversions of common chords. Practice them in all keys using all nine types of seventh chords.

TRACK 4

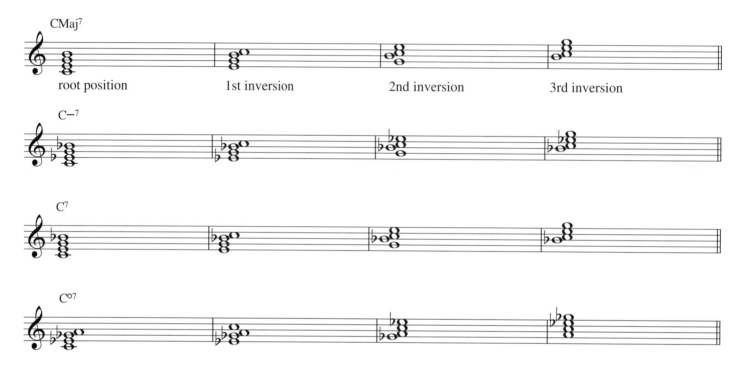

Fig. 2.1. Seventh Chords in Root Position and Inversions

Major and Minor 6 Chords

The major 6 chord is a major triad with an additional major 6 interval from the root of the chord. The minor 6 is a minor triad with an added major 6 from the root. These chords function like seventh chords in a chord progression and often substitute for the major 7. Their inversions are formed the same way as with seventh chords.

Practice 2.1. Seventh Chord Voicings

TRACK 4

Listen to the chords on the audio track, and then play them.

Use figure 2.1 to practice these chords with their inversions in all twelve keys. Divide them up, and practice different types in all twelve keys, every day, in all inversions.

CLOSE VOICINGS AND OPEN VOICINGS

Four-note chords voiced within an octave are called *four-way close-position* voicings. This is to distinguish them from *open-position*, or "spread," voicings, which contain intervals of a fourth or greater. (Open voicings can also contain close intervals but must contain intervals of a fourth or greater.) Play these voicings and note the difference in the sound.

TRACK 5

(a) Close Voicings

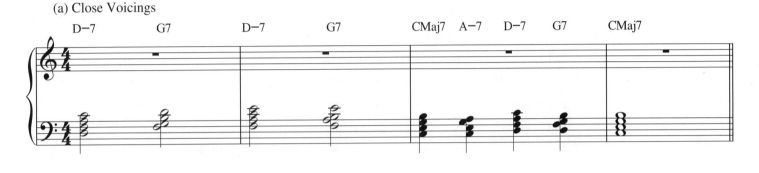

(b) Open Voicings

Fig. 2.2. Close and Open Voicings. (a) Close voicings are built up from the bottom in thirds or less. (b) Open voicings include intervals built in fourths or greater.

Practice 2.2. Close/Open Voicing Practice

TRACK 5

Listen to the chords on the audio track, then play, using figure 2.2 as a reference.

It's very important to practice and memorize the seventh chords in all keys and inversions since they form the basis of more complicated voicings. The inversions are important in order to facilitate smooth voice leading (lesson 3).

Voice Leading

Voice leading is a performance practice where the goal is to move as smoothly as possible from one chord to the next. By learning how to voice lead chords properly, you will not only be able to play chord changes with greater ease but also create a more pleasing sound for your listener. Figure 3.1 shows two voice-led progressions beginning on different inversions.

Listen to this example, and then practice it along with the recording.

TRACK 6

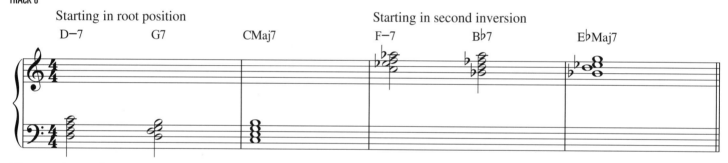

Fig. 3.1. Smooth Voice Leading

RULES OF SMOOTH VOICE LEADING

For smooth transitions between chords, follow these voice-leading rules. As an example, we will use a progression of D–7 to G7.

1. Repeat common tones. In figure 3.2, the common tones found in both chords are D and F, while the other notes change to create the new chord.

2. Move each voice by a half step or a whole step. In figure 3.2, the notes that change are arrived at by stepwise motion. C moves down to B, and A moves down to G.

TRACK 7

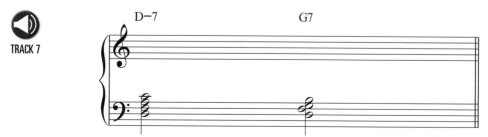

Fig. 3.2. Common Tones and Stepwise Motion

3. Use the closest inversion of the next chord unless it is too low. In figure 3.3, the E♭Maj7 voicing is too low, resulting in a "muddy" or unclear sound.

TRACK 8

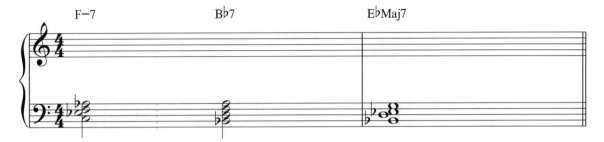

Fig. 3.3. Low Voicing

Figure 3.4 shows a better option for voice leading this progression. Now, the E♭Maj7 voicing is clear, and the sound is more recognizable.

TRACK 9

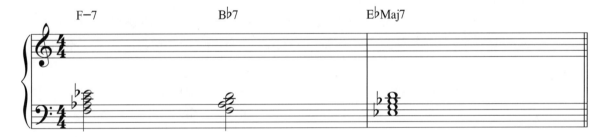

Fig. 3.4. Voice Leading Alternative

After mastering these voice-leading rules, you can then begin to implement them into your playing. Figure 3.5 shows how to voice lead chords while also playing a melody.

TRACK 10

Fig. 3.5. Voice Leading with Melody

Getting Away from Root Position: Expanded Shell Voicings

The tendency of beginning players is to rely on root position chords because they are readily identifiable with their roots on the bottom. But to continue playing this way prevents you from learning voice leading, which is why it is essential to practice using inversions.

The next step is to change the order of the chord tones with expanded shell voicings. *Expanded shell* voicings allow you to use two hands to play a single chord voicing.

The *shell* of a seventh chord is root + 7 or root + 3 in the left hand.

The *expanded shell* contains root + 7 or root + 3 in the left hand and 3 + 5 in the right hand.

Practice 4.1. Expanded Shell Voicings

Listen to the expanded shell voicings on the recording, following along with figure 4.1, which uses them in II V I progressions through all twelve keys. Then, play along with the recording.

TRACK 11

Fig. 4.1. II V I Expanded Shells with Two Hands

Practice 4.2. Two-Hand Comping behind a Soloist

Figure 4.2 is an example of how to use expanded shells and open voicings to comp for a soloist. On the recording, a guitar is playing the solo with a rhythm section. Play these chord voicings to comp behind the soloist.

TRACK 12   TRACK 13

Fig. 4.2. Expanded Shells and Open Voicings

Tensions

Tensions are upper extensions of seventh chords. They are found by raising the 2nd, 4th, and 6th degrees of the major scale of the root key up one octave and are then called 9, 11, and 13. Tensions can be raised and lowered (or "altered"), as in ♯11 or ♭13.

The following chart summarizes the tensions typically added to the main types of seventh chords in jazz.

TENSIONS

Major 7	9 ♯11 13
Minor 7	9 11 13
Minor 7♭5	9 11 ♭13
Augmented 7	9 ♯11
Dominant 7	♭9 9 ♯9 ♯11 ♭13 13
Major 6	9 ♯11
Minor 6	9 11
Diminished 7	any note a whole step above a chord tone

In diatonic harmony, only certain tensions are typically used on each type of seventh chord. This is because some tensions will create harsh-sounding dissonances on the chord.

Here is an example:

TRACK 14

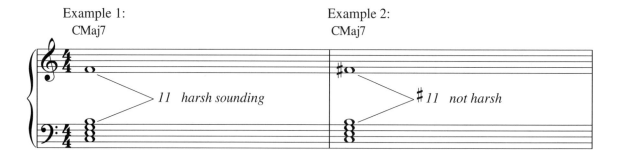

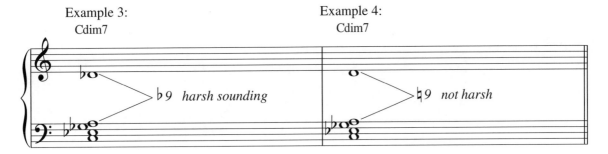

Fig. 5.1. Allowable Tensions

Example 1 in figure 5.1 uses a natural 11 (F). The flat 9 interval created between E and F is harsh sounding. By changing the tension to a ♯11 (F♯), as in example 2, we create a natural 9 interval that sounds much less harsh. Similarly, example 3 uses flat 9 as the tension, thus creating a flat 9 interval between C and D♭. By instead using natural 9 (D) as the tension, as in example 4, a much more pleasant natural 9 interval is created.

As the name implies, these notes add *tension*, color, and interest to the chords. Chords with one or more tensions have an unresolved quality. If they are dominant 7ths, they tend to demand resolution to their related tonic chord, as in V7 to IMaj7. However, in a blues, the final I7 chord can (and often does) contain tensions that remain unresolved, such as C7 (9, ♯11,13; see lesson 20).

Note: T9 is considered to be very stable when it is on a IMaj7, I–Maj7, or I7 chord but not as stable when on a V7 chord. "Stable" means that the chord is at a point of rest or resolution.

In chord symbols, tensions are usually indicated in parentheses, but the parentheses are sometimes eliminated in old fake books and lead sheets.

Practice 5.1. How Tensions Resolve

Listen to the chords on the audio track, then play. Note the use of expanded shell voicings (see lesson 4).

TRACK 15

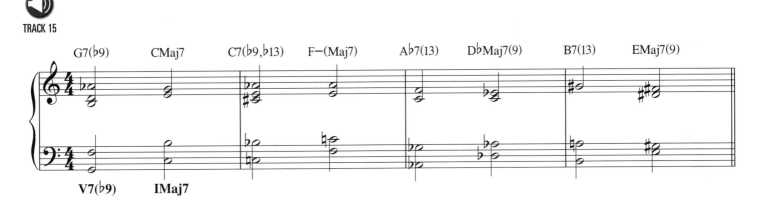

Fig. 5.2. How Tensions Resolve

Comping with Steps Using Guide Tones and Tensions

Guide tones are the third (or sus4) and seventh of any seventh chord. They (plus the root) are required for a chord to be recognizable as a seventh chord. The pianist does not always have to play the root because, in an ensemble, the bassist will play it. If you are playing solo, you can either play a root in the left hand, then jump to the guide tones, or play no roots—just the chord—and the melody or solo will either provide or imply the chord root. The fifth is also often omitted from seventh-chord voicings.

Here are three options for comping with guide tones. To introduce the use of tensions in your chord voicings, you can play:

1. a left-hand voicing containing guide tones only

2. a left-hand voicing with guide tones plus one tension (9 or 13)

3. a left-hand voicing with guide tones plus one tension and the root played in the right hand, either as a single note or in octaves.

The next series of examples illustrates comping with guide tones using these different approaches. Only use option 3 after you have mastered options 1 and 2, playing along with tracks 16 to 18 at tempo. Later, you will use these three approaches to comp on a 12-bar blues (see lesson 20).

Practice 6.1. Guide Tone Comping

Listen to the three examples on tracks 16 to 18, and then play them.

TRACK 16

1. Guide tones only in the left hand (no right hand)

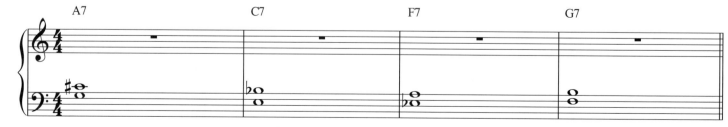

Fig. 6.1. Comping with Guide Tones

2. Guide tones plus one tension in the left hand

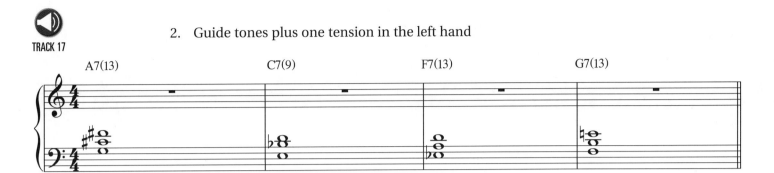

Fig. 6.2. Guide Tones Plus One Tension

3. Guide tones plus one tension in the left hand, root in the right hand (root can be played in octaves)

Fig. 6.3. Guide Tones Plus One Tension (LH) and Root (RH)

If you follow this approach, you will learn that the guide tones, or the guide tones plus tensions in the left hand, provide good voicing options when comping a solo played in the right hand. It is also consistent with post-bebop jazz piano styles. For example, there are numerous examples of Bill Evans using guide tones only or "guide tones plus one" tension in the left hand when soloing.

Beginning pianists are often taught to play the same voicing in both hands (e.g., C E G B/C E G B). This method is not particularly valuable because in real-life playing situations, this almost never occurs. Guide tones are more useful in an ensemble and sound more professional. With this three-step approach, you first learn to use left-hand guide tones, then apply a tension, and finally add the root (possibly in octaves) in the right hand to create a larger voicing for two hands (see lesson 10).

Four-Way Close Voicings with Tension Substitutions

In lesson 2, I defined four-way close-position voicings using the four chord tones of a seventh chord within an octave. The distinctive sound of jazz four-way close voicings is achieved with tension substitutions (e.g., tension 9 for the root and tension 13 for the 5th). These voicings have two configurations, commonly called "A" and "B" position.

The reason for two positions ("A" and "B") is to facilitate smooth voice leading in a chord progression. In position "A," the 3rd of the II–7 chord is on the bottom. In position "B," the 7 of the II–7 chord is on the bottom.

The "A" and "B" position voicings were developed by bebop pianists like Red Garland and Bill Evans just as the acoustic bass was replacing the pianist's left hand in playing the roots of chords. Therefore, the voicings are rootless because the bassist is expected to play the roots of the chords, thus freeing the pianist to incorporate tensions into a left-hand voicing.

There is a formula for each position. I have illustrated this formula with II V I progressions. Notice the smooth voice leading, and practice transposing it to all twelve keys.

TRACK 19

Here is the "A" position II V I formula:

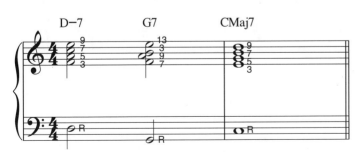

Fig. 7.1. Rootless Voicings with T9 and T13, "A" Position II V I Formula

TRACK 20

Here is the "B" position II V I formula:

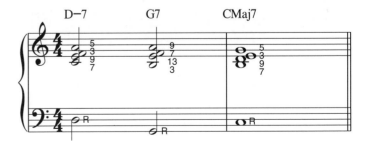

Fig. 7.2. Rootless Voicings with T9 and T13, "B" Position II V I Formula

Practice 7.1. A and B Position Voicing Practice

Listen to the "A" and "B" position voicings of the progression in figures 7.1 and 7.2 (tracks 19 and 20), and then practice them.

It is important not to play the voicings in a range that is too low. If a voicing sounds "muddy," raise it up an octave. In some keys, position "B" voicings sound good in either octave, though they are generally set higher than "A" position voicings.

Sometimes, these voicings are referred to (inaccurately) as "6, 9" voicings. They should be referred to as "9, 13" rootless voicings, since it is not the 6 (a chord tone) but tension 13 that is substituted for the 5th of the chord. Tension 9 substitutes for the root of the chord.

Practice 7.2. "A" and "B" Position Voicings

These voicings can be played with either hand. If there is no bassist to play the roots under the voicings, then the keyboard player can play the root in the left hand and the voicings in the right hand.

Listen to these progressions on track 21, and then play them.

TRACK 21

"A" position

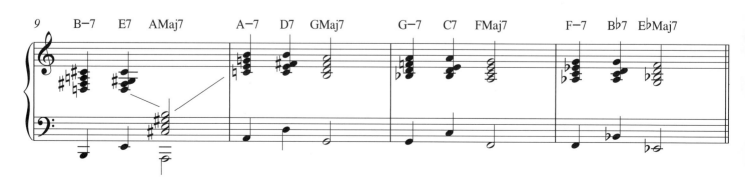

"B" position

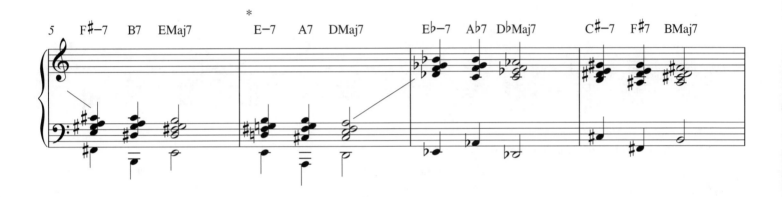

Fig. 7.3. "A" and "B" Position Voicings with Two Hands, with Root in LH. Tension substitutions: 9 for R and 13 for 5

* This chord progression is written one octave lower than it is played on the recording. It can be played in either range.

TRACK 22

Fig. 7.4. II V I Rootless with 9 and 13, LH

ADDING THE RIGHT HAND

Once you've had a lot of practice using these voicings in the LH only, you can then add two notes in the RH, creating a 6-note, two-handed voicing. Most students find it easy to play a chord tone or tension in octaves in the RH. This way, you have a voicing that is rootless in the LH, with tension substitutions (the bass player in an ensemble plays the roots of the chords) with two notes (doubling) in the RH, making it a "complete" chord. It will sound very rich and full.

Another option for the RH is to play the 5th in octaves, or T9 + 5 and T13 + T9.

Practice 7.3. RH Octaves: Chord Tone or Tension

Listen to the progression in figure 7.5 (track 23), and then practice it in all keys.

TRACK 23

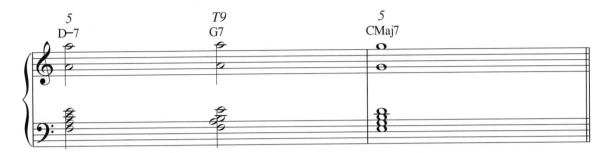

Fig. 7.5. 9,13 LH Rootless with 5 and T9 in RH

In figure 7.5, notice that there is smooth voice leading in the RH from D–7 to G7 (II–7 V7). The same note (A) is used, which is the 5 of D–7 and T9 of G7. The right hand then moves down stepwise to G, the 5 of CMaj7.

Including tensions 9 and 13 adds color to the chord. It may take you a while to get used to the sound if you haven't listened to much jazz piano (see "Discography"). If this is the case, you might prefer to play the voicings in the right hand and the roots in the left hand. Practice them both ways. The emphasis in this book is on playing these voicings with the left hand so that the right hand is free to add notes for two-handed comping.

Figure 7.6 demonstrates the use of chord tones and tensions in the right hand while playing II V I of C in the "A" position in the left hand. Remember, these voicings are designed for use when a bassist will play the roots below the piano voicing. It gives the pianist a lot more flexibility.

TRACK 24

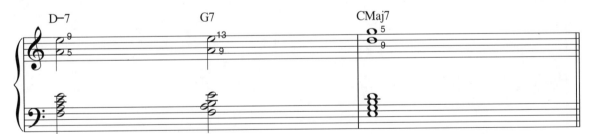

Fig. 7.6. LH Plays 9,13 Rootless Voicings; RH Plays 5, 9,13

Practice 7.4. Create "B" Position

Listen to the progression in figure 7.6 (track 24), and then practice it. Transpose it to all keys, and then use the "B" position in the left hand while playing the same chord tones and tensions in the right hand.

You should have the goal of memorizing "A" and "B" position voicings in all keys. The more you use them, the faster you will memorize them!

Voicings in Fourths

Fourths voicings are derived from a style of jazz piano whose chief architect is the great jazz pianist McCoy Tyner, who in addition to heading his own trio, is famous for his work with John Coltrane and Wayne Shorter. (Listen to the McCoy Tyner Trio CD *Reaching Fourth*.) The result of playing fourths is an open sound that works well against pentatonic scales.

Practice the following examples along with the piano track on the recording.

For example, in C Dorian (bottom staff), starting on C, build a fourths voicing on each degree of the mode. You must restrict yourself to only the notes in C Dorian. In other words, you can only use C, D, Eb, F, G, A, and Bb in your voicings. So, from the bottom up in the LH, you have C, F, Bb, then D, G, C, then Eb, A, D, then F, Bb, Eb, and so on.

TRACK 25

Fig. 8.1. Fourths Voicings in C Dorian

Practice 8.1. Fourths Voicings

Listen to track 25, and then play the progression in figure 8.1. Play the fourths voicings based on each degree of C Dorian (in order). Then, transpose it into F Dorian, and do the same thing. Practice cycling between two or three different fourths voicings in sequence. When you are good at this, add two more notes in the right hand for a two-handed voicing, such as 3 + 5, 5 + R, and 7 + 3.

Practice 8.2. Fourths Voicing Transposition Practice

Listen to the progression on track 26, and then play it. Transpose into all keys. All notes should be from the Dorian mode built on the first chord's root.

TRACK 26

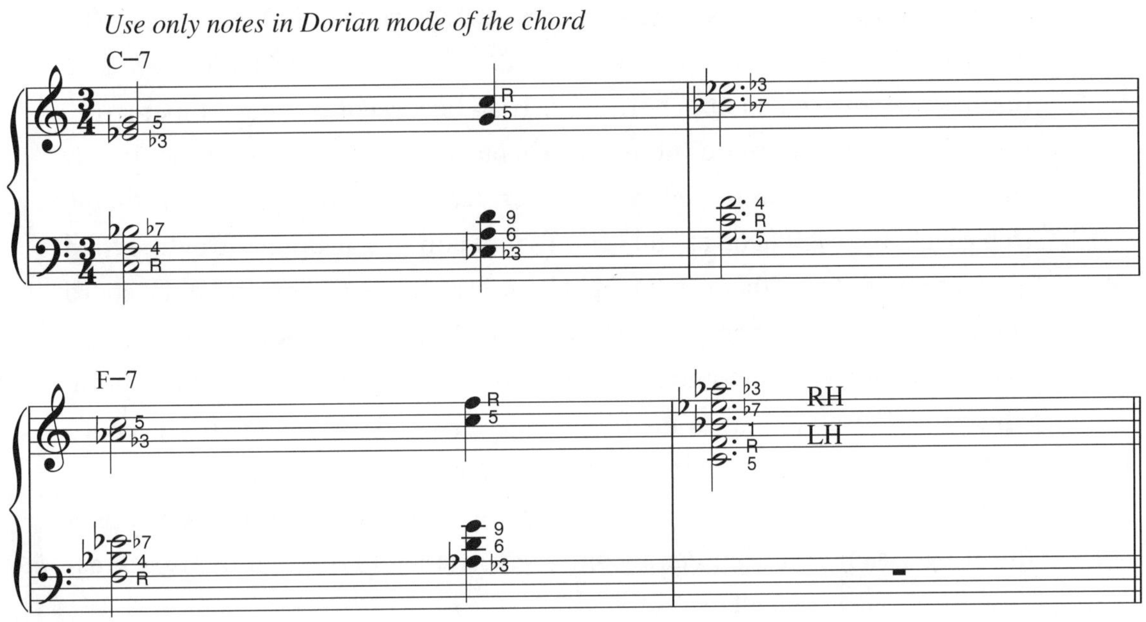

Fig. 8.2. Fourths Voicings for Two Hands

In addition to "Footprints" by Wayne Shorter, you can practice fourths on Miles Davis's tune "So What" (from *Kind of Blue*), which contains only two chords, D–7 and E♭–7, both of which are voiced in fourths.

LESSON 9

Upper-Structure Triads

Upper-structure triads are commonly found in modern jazz of the 1960s and can be easily played with tunes like "Footprints" and "So What."

All except four bars of the following chord progression are voicings in fourths. In bars 17–20, there are two bars of D7 (9,♯11,13) and two bars of D♭7 (9,♯11,13). These chords can also be called "E/D7" and "E♭/D♭7." The chord above the slash (/) is called an upper-structure triad because it contains upper structures of a seventh chord (tensions), which, played together, form a triad. In this case, the three tensions played together (9, ♯11, and 13) form a major triad in the treble clef. In the left hand are the chord's root and ♭7. The upper-structure triad is superimposed over them, in the right hand. The three tensions color the chord and make it unstable, needing to resolve. The E♭/D♭7 chord does resolve to C–7 (the I–7 of the key). Harmonically, this chord is ♭II7, a dominant-function chord, which means it functions in the progression like a V7. The name of the chord itself depends on its root, which is the bottom note of the voicing.

Practice figure 9.1 with track 27 (bass and drums only). Practice comping this progression until your ear becomes accustomed to the sound. Also, transpose the voicings into all twelve keys.

TRACK 27

CHORD PROGRESSION USING FOURTHS AND UPPER-STRUCTURE TRIADS

Fig. 9.1. Upper-Structure Triads and Fourths

Open-Position Voicings

Open voicings are voicings for two hands in which the intervals are in fourths or greater. Thirds can be used in the right hand. The result is a very different sound from the sound of four-way close-position voicings. Practice the same chord in open and close position and observe how they are different.

The basic difference between the open-position left-hand approach and the four-way close voicings is that there are wider intervals between notes. If you follow these guidelines, you will automatically have fourths, fifths, and sevenths in the left hand.

The right hand has several choices:

- chord tones missing (not played) in the left hand, such as R or 5 or both

- chord tones or tensions played in octaves

- doubling the root, a chord tone, or a tension in octaves and playing another chord tone or tension in between

- one chord tone + one or two tensions (such as 9 and 13) or two chord tones

Figure 10.1 contains some typical open voicings. Listen (track 28), and then play them along with the rhythm track.

TRACK 28

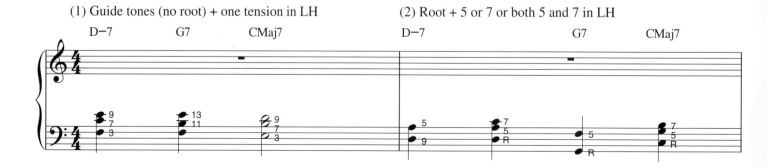

Open Position (Spread) Voicings RH positions added

(1) Chord tones missing (not played) in LH

(2) Tension 11 played in octves
(3) 3rd played in octaves

(4) T9 in octaves

(5) Doubling the root, a chord tone, or tension in octaves and playing another chord tone in between

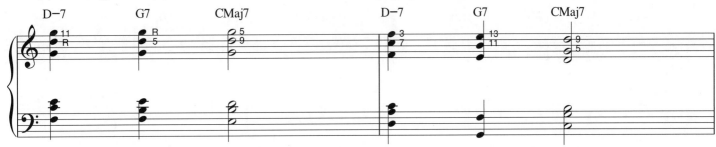

(6) One chord tone + one tension or two tensions (such as 9 and 13) or two chord tones

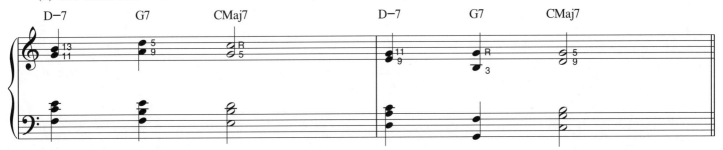

Fig. 10.1 Open Voicings

Figure 10.2 is a comping score (two hands playing chord voicings only) with open voicings. Listen to track 29, then play. Practice and memorize the voicings. Analyzing the voicings for chord tones and tensions is also a great learning device. Make it a habit to do this with jazz scores. Make a photocopy of the score, and write in the chord tones and tensions. (See lesson 12 for how to label voicings.)

TRACK 29 TRACK 30

OPEN VOICINGS WITH TENSIONS
(CHORD PROGRESSION)

10.2. Open-Position Voicings with Tensions (Chord Progression). These chord changes are common in jazz.

Work with chord voicings written as a score, to supplement your lead sheet playing, with the goal of memorizing open-position voicings and getting used to using them so that you can think of them quickly when comping. Open-position voicings can be played in two ways:

1.   guide tones (no root) + one tension in LH

2.   root + 7 or both 5 and 7 in LH.

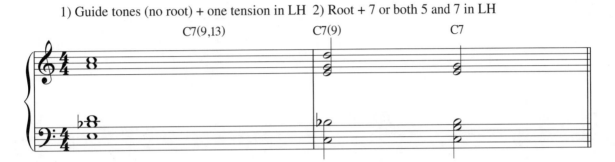

Fig. 10.3. Two Ways to Play Open Voicings

The experienced pianist will use both voicing types when comping. Open voicings are particularly useful when playing solo piano and a full, orchestrated sound is desired. When playing solo piano, open voicings can be alternated with more sparse voicings, such as guide tones in the left hand or guide tones with one tension.

"Blue in Purple" is a good piece to work on for two-hand open voicings. It's challenging because there are lots of tensions on the chords. The voicings in this arrangement are typical examples of open voicings for two hands used in jazz. They give the music its characteristic dark coloring.

Listen to track 31. Analyze each chord for chord tones and tensions. Include melody notes: often they are tensions on the chords. Label the chord tones and tensions by writing them in this book. Then, play along with the recording.

TRACK 31   TRACK 32

Blue in Purple

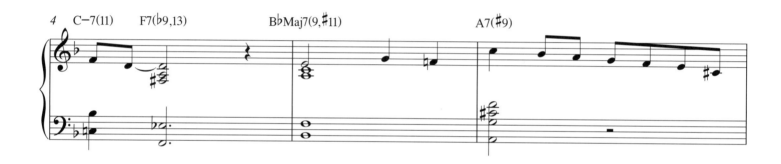

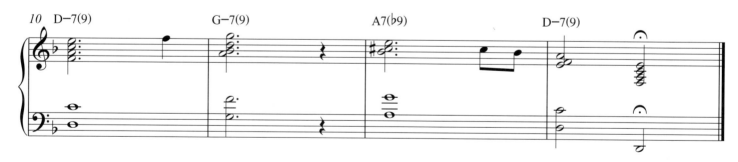

Fig. 10.4. "Blue in Purple." Note: Use the damper pedal to sustain chords that you can't reach to play all notes simultaneously.

LESSON 11

Combining Four-Way Close Voicings with Open Voicings

When you practice this exercise, you will notice that not all of the chord voicings are open. Some are constructed with four-way close voicings with tension substitutions in the left hand and open voicings in the right hand (usually voiced in fourths). They are large voicings with five to seven notes.

This is done to create contrast and interest. There is nothing wrong with using all open voicings; however, your comping will take on a more interesting character if you always think about contrast and include some close voicings also.

Practice this progression. Label all chord tones and tensions.

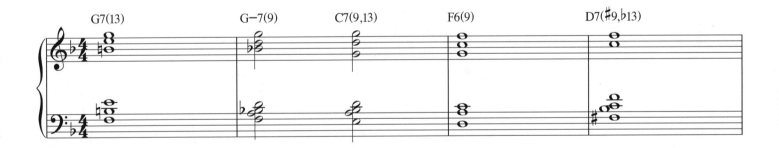

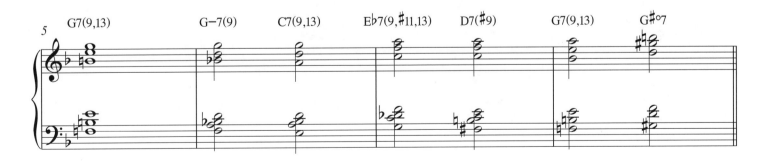

Fig. 11.1. Open Voicings with Tensions (Advanced)

LESSON 12

More Comping Examples

This lesson is a series of comping examples that illustrate the concepts we have been studying. Follow a two-step process for each example.

Step 1. Analyze the voicings for chord tones and tensions (label them). Follow the voice leading, and notice the use of open and close voicings (contrast).

Step 2. Practice with track 33 and with a metronome (click on beats 2 and 4). You should *memorize* the chord voicings.

I have discussed the importance of analyzing chord voicings in lesson 10. Analyzing helps you memorize chord voicings, in all keys, that you can use over and over again. A great practice idea is to take a tune and write open voicings for each chord change on a piece of manuscript paper. Label the chords with chord names, and then label each chord tone and tension. Then, memorize the voicings. This is easier to do if you choose a tune you already know how to play.

TRACK 33

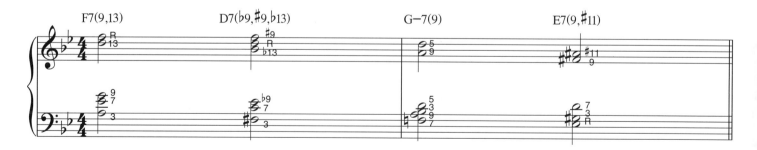

Fig. 12.1. Labeling the Chords with Chord Tones and Tensions

With the recording, practice playing these II V I open voicings with the rhythm section.

Label chord tones and tensions. Label the voicings, and practice with track 34.

TRACK 34

Chord Voicings for Two Hands

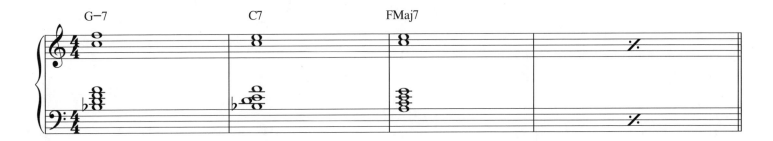

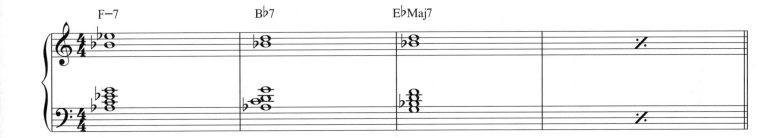

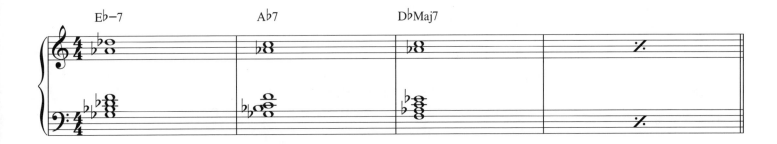

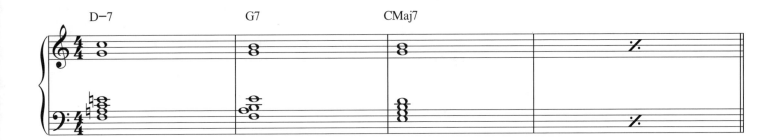

Fig. 12.2. Chord Progression 1: II V I, Two Hands

Listen, then play. Label chord tones and tensions in figure 12.3. Label the voicings, and practice with the rhythm section on the recording.

TRACK 35   TRACK 36

Jazz Blues for Two Hands

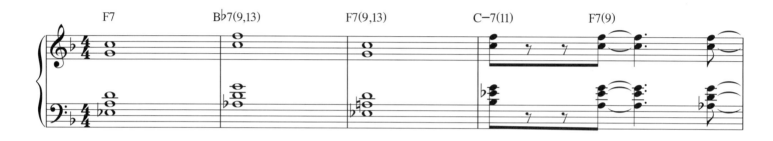

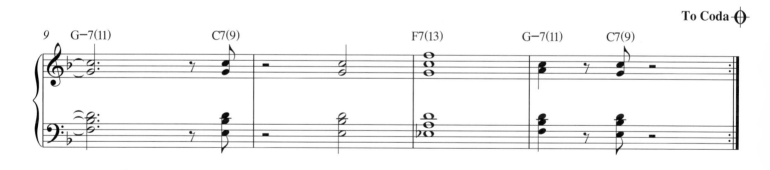

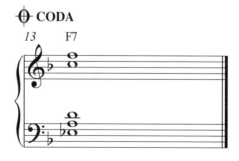

Fig. 12.3. Chord Progression 2: Jazz Blues, Two Hands

Rhythms: Syncopation

In comping, the piano is functioning as a percussion instrument, even though it is simultaneously playing its role as a harmony instrument. As such, a pianist must become familiar with various common comping rhythms found in jazz styles. It is also important to be familiar with comping patterns used in rock and other styles of music. Comping can mean using block chords or arpeggiating them, or it can mean incorporating block chords and arpeggios to create musical textures. A rhythm can also be used to create or enhance a mood. In this lesson, we will examine the use of rhythms in several different styles of music.

FEEL AND GROOVE

A *feel* is the rhythmic subdivision. A *groove* is the whole composite accompaniment, including feel, but also, notes, chord figures, background licks, style, and accents.

The way a rhythm is played is called *articulation*. When a beat is subdivided, it is important that the subdivisions be played, or counted (when held), evenly.

Different musical styles incorporate different and distinctive rhythmic feels. For example, swing jazz and rock shuffle beats contain a syncopated eighth-note feel, while bossa nova and many styles of rock contain an even eighth-note feel.

Syncopation

Straight-ahead jazz swing tunes have a syncopated, or "swing," eighth-note feel.

Syncopation occurs in two ways. The first way is internal to the beat. Figure 13.1 shows how the first two eighth notes in a triplet are tied to create syncopation. Eighth notes in jazz or swing time must be played as jazz eighth notes.

Fig. 13.1. Jazz Eighth-Note Feel

The third eighth note in the triplet is heavily accented, creating a strong pulse on what would otherwise be a weaker part of the beat. The upbeat (as this final eighth note is called) is stronger than the downbeat (the first eighth note of the beat, or in this case, the first two eighths of the triplet, tied). The word *syncopation* comes from the Latin word meaning "to swoon," and the term *syncope* is used in medicine to describe fainting. Figuratively speaking, the upbeat is "fainting," or "falling over," into the next downbeat.

The second way that syncopation occurs is within the phrase. When upbeat attacks are surrounded by rests, syncopation occurs.

Fig. 13.2. Upbeat Attacks Surrounded by Rests 1

Fig. 13.3. Upbeat Attacks Surrounded by Rests 2

Syncopation in the phrase also occurs when dotted notes, accents, and ties are used. Here is an example combining upbeat attacks surrounded by rests, dotted notes, accents, and ties.

Fig. 13.4. Syncopation with Dotted Notes

In swing jazz, *forward motion* is achieved with syncopation. Without it, melodies and improvised lines tend to be dull and static. Notice the syncopation in the melody to "Blues for Mr. H.C."

The chord changes for the solos can be comped with one or both hands. There are a lot of changes, so practice slowly.

The eighth notes you see written out in the melody on a lead sheet can be played either as even eighths or syncopated, or "swing," eighths. The only way you can know which way to play them (they don't look any different from each other) is to know the style of the tune or to get the information from the lead sheet, which may or may not be there. It's usually to the left of the page under the song title, as shown in "Blues for Mr. H.C."

Listen to the band track for "Blues for Mr. H.C." The piano plays the head, and then the guitar player takes a solo on the changes. Comp along with the guitar solo using the rhythms in figure 13.6. Use any chord voicing for one or two hands.

TRACK 37   TRACK 38

Blues for Mr. H.C.

Fig. 13.5. "Blues for Mr. H.C."

Fig. 13.6. Comping Rhythms for "Blues for Mr. H.C."

GROOVE

A groove is the whole composite accompaniment, including feel, but also notes, chord figures, background licks, style, and accents. There are many types of grooves, both within styles of jazz and in other forms of music. In any type of groove, it's important that the pianist's comping fits in and does not detract from or destroy the melody. A groove provides support for and enhances the melodic line.

Groove vs. Anti-groove

The concept of "anti-groove" is best illustrated using swing feel. Some students have trouble with swing feel and comp on beats 1 and 3 instead of 2 and 4. This is sometimes referred to as "anti-groove." To correct this, practice comping with a metronome with the clicks on beats 2 and 4. Start with slow tempos and gradually increase to fast tempos. This kind of practice will improve your comping dramatically. Later, you can practice comping on the "and" of beat 2 and the "and" of beat 4 (upbeats).

Fig. 13.7. Groove Example

Fig.13.8. Anti-Groove Example

Comping with Bass and Drums

The *rhythm section* is composed of piano, bass, and drums (or guitar, bass, and drums). In lesson 13, emphasis was placed on the importance of the groove in comping. In the various jazz styles, the groove is always foremost.

HOW TO LOCK IN WITH A GROOVE IN DIFFERENT STYLES AND METERS

In this lesson, we will examine written examples of various rhythmic grooves. The piano comping part indicates where the pianist should comp in order to lock in with the bass and drums.

You will notice that the piano often comps the same basic rhythm but that the bass and drums play different basic rhythms depending on the style. The characteristic jazz or swing eighth-note feel played on the cymbal is the basis for basic Swing rhythm.

Fig. 14.1. Basic Swing Rhythm

Here are some examples of how to lock in with the groove. Listen, and then play with the tracks first with the full band tracks and then on the tracks without a keyboard. (Use any chord to comp.)

TRACK 39   TRACK 40

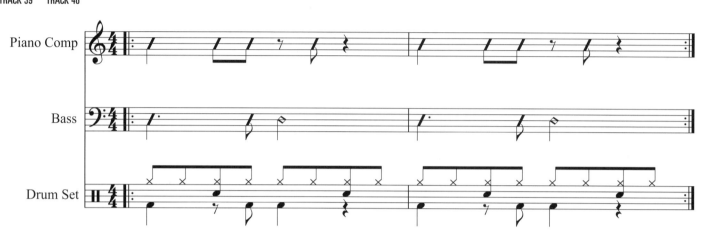

Fig. 14.2. Standard Rock (Even Eighths)

TRACK 41   TRACK 42

Fig. 14.3. Bossa Nova

TRACK 43   TRACK 44

Fig. 14.4. Swing

Fig. 14.5. Standard Rock (R&B)

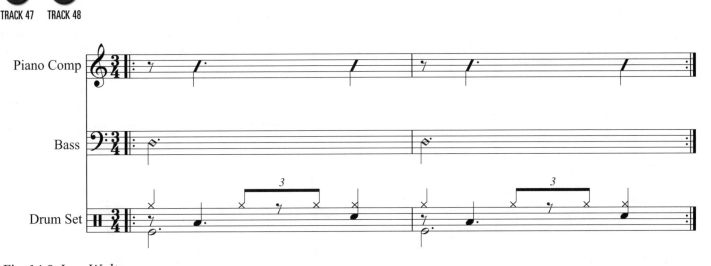

Fig. 14.6. Jazz Waltz

There are many variations on these six basic grooves. It's important to learn the pulse and rhythmic feel of a groove and to count along with the beat in each measure. Many jazz tunes derive their groove from rock or bossa nova, which is why you should practice comping with all six grooves in figures 14.2 through 14.6.

In figure 14.7, the comping follows the melody, which establishes a strong swing groove. The guitar plays the melody. Comp on "Groove Tune" along with the rhythm track on the recording, and practice locking in with the groove by playing the rhythms exactly as written.

Groove Tune

Fig. 14.7. "Groove Tune"

There are other music styles (including the jazz ballad) in which the groove is subtler, composed of textures, arpeggiations, and fragmentations of the chord. This type of piano accompaniment can span a range of several octaves. Some comping follows the melody line more than others.

TEXTURES (ARPEGGIATION AND FRAGMENTATION)

As a rule, the pianist does not repeat (double) the melody line in comping. In jazz ballads, chords are voiced so as to complement and support the soloist (for example, a vocalist or horn player).

Figure 14.8 is a jazz or rock ballad in which textures (arpeggiation and fragmentation) are appropriate. Block chords are often interspersed with arpeggios. Listen to the accompaniment by itself first, then to the guitar playing a solo over the chord changes. Notice how the textures complement the melody.

TRACK 51

Fig.14.8. "Jazz Ballad" Comping Using Textures, Arpeggiation, Fragmentation, and Block Chords

Comping with a Guitarist

I led my own trio at the Four Seasons Hotel in Boston for nineteen years. When I began playing there in 1985, I played very safely, very inside (using chord scales to play over the original changes). It was all I knew how to do, and it was what the management wanted. I practiced comping so that I could play softly and still swing. The management would change the band format from time to time. Most of the time it was piano, bass, and drums, but sometimes it would be piano, bass, and horn; or piano, bass, and guitar (no drums). So I adapted. I lined up several of the greatest horn players around to play with my bassist and me—a different featured artist each week in rotation. Playing with great horn players really improved my comping. I also played with Mitch Seidman, a great guitar player who teaches in Berklee's Ear Training Department. Mitch is featured on the recordings included with this book, demonstrating how a pianist and guitarist take turns comping in a quartet.

If there is a guitarist or other chording instrument in the band, the pianist should take turns comping with him or her. Alternating choruses or half choruses is the easiest way. Piano and guitar comping simultaneously almost always results in muddiness, and excess playing in general detracts from the groove. I've found that it is very rare that a guitar and piano, or keyboard, comping together at the same time sounds good. So Mitch and I would take turns comping. Sometimes, I'd lay out and let him comp during solos. Other times, I'd comp while he soloed. Sometimes he'd comp for me during my solos. We got so that we barely had to glance at one another to know what we were going to do.

Listen to track 52 where guitar and piano take turns comping for a bass solo. This is a listening track, so comping along with the pianist is optional.

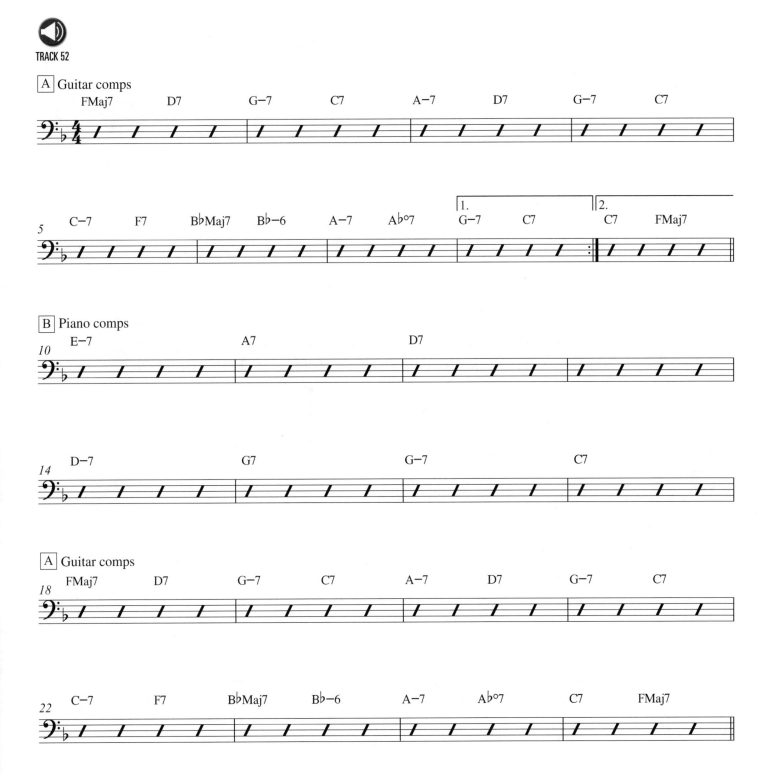

Fig. 15.1. Guitar and Piano Taking Turns Comping for Bass Solo (Rhythm Changes)

If you're in a group with a guitar player and horn player(s), you have to be circumspect. You have to establish eye contact with the guitar player so that you can take turns comping for the horn and the bass player. I really like the sound of guitar comping for acoustic bass. I don't know why, maybe because it is strings with strings, but I often let the guitar player comp for the bassist. Always, always, think about the entire sound. Remember that you are part of the rhythm section, even though you are playing a melody and harmony instrument.

LESSON 16

Comping behind Your Own Solo

When you are the soloist, you have the option of comping in your left hand while you play a line in the right hand, or you can opt to play no chords at all (just right-hand lines). The range of the melody dictates which chord voicings to use. When you comp in the left hand, your chords should drive the right-hand solo rhythmically. Listen to Bill Evans for great examples of this.

Think about the dual functions of comping: comping for yourself and comping behind another soloist. When comping behind another soloist, the pianist can choose to use the left hand only or to comp with two hands.

TRACK 53

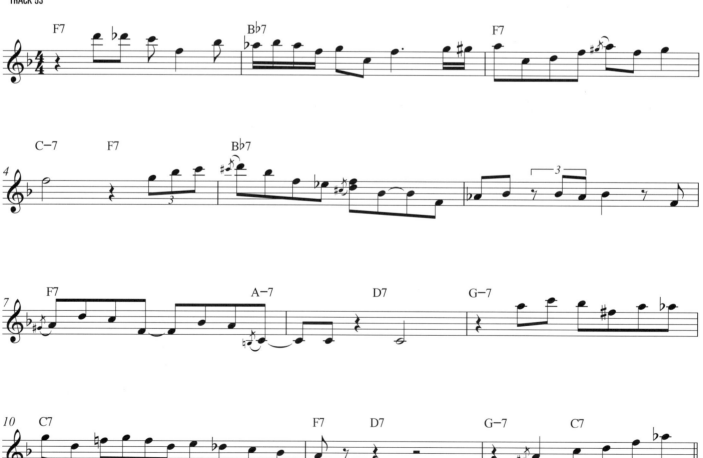

Fig. 16.1. Comping with LH while Playing Line in RH

Contrast between comping and not comping in the left hand during your solo is important. I let my left hand drop out when soloing if I feel the situation calls for it. If you listen to Herbie Hancock's acoustic playing, you will hear that he does this a lot. So do Keith Jarrett and Brad Mehldau. This expands the range of my soloing right hand. I can go into "left hand comping" territory and make use of the entire keyboard in my melody lines. It also frees me up to reharmonize on the spot and enter uncharted territory. Listen to track 54. Contrast left hand comping with dropping out.

TRACK 54

(right hand)

Fig.16.2. Comping with LH and Dropping out LH to Solo with RH

LESSON 17

Comping Strategies

In every playing situation, your comping decisions or strategies should be based on complementing/supporting the soloist in order to make that soloist sound as good as possible.

As you gain experience in comping, you will be in many different playing situations, which require different types of comping and different approaches to comping. The decision not to comp, if called for, can be as important as comping. Certain jazz styles require assertive and rhythmic comping, and others require a more Spartan approach. There are some general guidelines to follow that are useful to keep in mind. The inexperienced/student soloist often needs to be fed chords in an assertive rhythmic pattern so that he or she can confidently stay in the groove. A vocalist with a piano accompanist, either with or without a group, needs the support of chords, unless performing a very modern or avant-garde repertoire.

PROVIDING SUPPORT AND ENHANCING THE SOLOIST'S MELODY LINE

If the soloist plays a lot of downbeats, comp with upbeat attacks to create forward motion.

TRACK 55

*Occasional downbeats add contrast

Fig. 17.1. Soloist Plays Downbeats

If the soloist plays long phrases, comp with syncopation for contrast.

TRACK 56

Fig. 17.2. Soloist Plays Long Phrases. Note: The guitar on the recording plays an octave higher than written.

If the soloist plays short (1- to 2-bar) phrases, punctuate with comping where appropriate (sparingly).

TRACK 57

Fig. 17.3. Soloist Plays Short Phrases

Listen to the tracks that correspond with figures 17.1 through 17.3. These are listening tracks. The guitar plays the solos, and the piano comps.

It's a good idea to comp during the first couple of choruses of any solo. Often, an advanced soloist will play more conventionally on the chord changes for several choruses and then will diverge from the chord changes, melody, rhythm, or all three. In these situations, comping can get in the way of the free flow of the soloist's ideas. Many soloists prefer the pianist to *lay out* (not play) during their solo. Some soloists will tell you this in advance, but others will not. Experience in judging where the soloist is going will enable you to determine when not to comp.

Trading fours is when a soloist plays for four bars, followed by the drummer playing a solo for four bars, followed by that same soloist again, or another soloist, alternating again with the drummer for one or more choruses. *Trading ones, twos, and eights* is also common. In most situations, trading with a drummer means the pianist should not comp behind the soloist. It tends to detract from the short statement being made by the soloist.

The advanced comping student should practice laying out during a solo. This sounds like advice from a Zen Buddhist, but consider the fact that you will be comping a lot more than you will be laying out. This is something that cannot be taught. Knowledge of styles and good taste are key. In your role as a comping instrument, you must never forget that, first and foremost, you are backing up and enhancing the soloist, providing support when needed, and not getting in the way of the soloist by playing too much. Sometimes this means not playing at all.

Comping in an Ensemble

If you have not done so already, you should start or join a group and have regular jam sessions in which you can practice comping, or take an ensemble class, if you are a student. You can sequence for yourself any number of tunes to practice in a band without keyboard format. This is an excellent way to practice, but it stops short of creating a real-life playing situation, one in which you need to pick up cues, establish eye contact with other players, and above all, learn to listen peripherally.

Peripheral Listening

All musicians should train their peripheral listening skills. Peripheral listening means that you are listening to the other players as carefully as you are listening to yourself play, observing the balance and the interplay. It requires that you divide your ear/brain so that you can do both at once. Most musicians have to work at this. All great compers are great peripheral listeners. The most important thing is that the entire sound of the band is good. And often, unless you are playing with your own band, you will have to adjust your soloing and comping to fit the entire sound.

Comping Rhythms Played with the Head (Hits)

The melody chorus of a tune is referred to as the *head*. It is the first chorus of a tune and usually states the melody as the composer wrote it. Some jazz musicians take extreme liberties with the original melody. Billie Holiday and Miles Davis are two examples of musicians who always diverged from the original melody on the head. (In fact, the way they performed the melody could be considered an improvised solo in itself.) The head is restated after all the musicians have taken a solo and signals that the tune will end when the final head ends.

Often, the head will contain hits that the pianist should comp to with the rest of the rhythm section. In "The Dragonfly," every melody note has a chord change hit. Where no hits are indicated, it's up to you to make the following decisions:

- How many attacks per bar/phrase?

- Accented or not accented?

- Loud or soft?

In general, the fewer hits, the better.

Listen, and then play using your own chord voicings to comp the rhythm hits with the rhythm track.

The Dragonfly

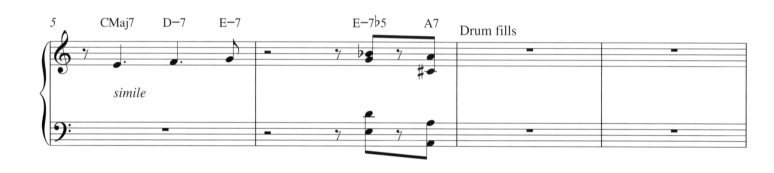

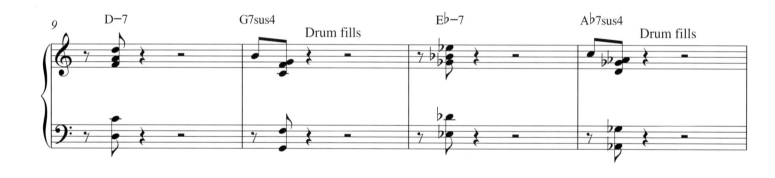

Fig. 18.1. "The Dragonfly"

AABA Song Form, 32-Bar Form

The 32-bar AABA song form and the 12-bar blues are often new to comping students. The final "A" in AABA form can cause confusion to some students who lose their place in the form when they first attempt to play three "A" sections in a row! To work on this specific problem, practice "The 'Standard' Standard" along with track 61, counting bars and developing a sense of what 2, 4, 8, and 16 bars feels like. When practicing the example in this lesson, interpret the chord symbols by using four-way close voicings and smooth voice leading (see lesson 3). Then, practice them with guide tones plus one (see lesson 6).

For "The 'Standard' Standard," first listen to the full quartet track, where the guitar plays the melody and the piano comps. Then, using the music minus one track, practice comping, counting bars as described above.

The "Standard" Standard

Fig. 19.1. "The 'Standard' Standard"

LESSON 20

12-Bar Blues 1, 2, 3

Here are two variations on a traditional 12-bar blues. First, listen to the full trio example (piano comping, bass, drums) of each variation, and notice the difference. Then, using the music minus one example (bass and drums only), practice them both in the key of C first, and then transpose to G, D, A, E, F, B♭, and E♭.

For "12-Bar Blues 1" (R&B 12/8), use this basic rhythm:

Fig. 20.1. 12-Bar Blues Rhythm

TRACK 62   TRACK 63

12/8 rhythm and blues feel

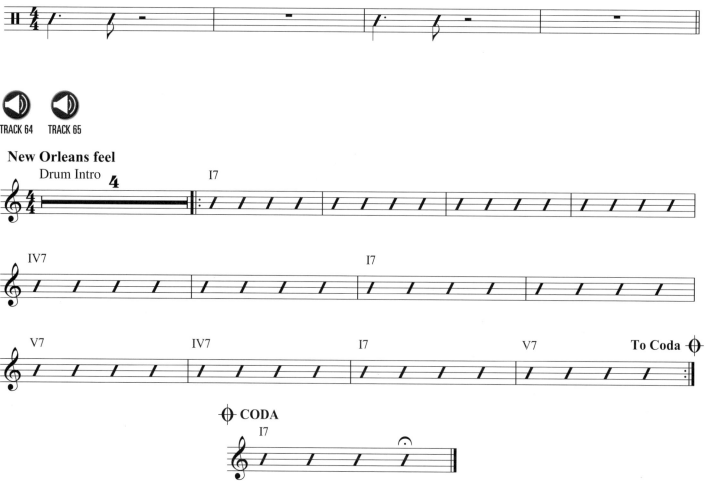

Fig. 20.1. 12-Bar Blues 1

For "12-Bar Blues 2" (New Orleans style), use this basic rhythm:

TRACK 64   TRACK 65

New Orleans feel

Fig. 20.2. 12-Bar Blues 2

12-BAR BLUES 3 (JAZZ VARIATION)

The jazz blues evolved from the traditional 12-bar blues. More harmony was added: II V of the IV chord going to IV (bar 4), and then II V of II–7 to II–7 (bar 8), then to V7/I, then I7.

The *turnaround* (two bars at the end of the form leading to the next chorus) is I7 V7/II II V7/I.

First listen to the full trio example (piano comping, bass, and drums). Then, using the track without keyboard (track 67), practice the example in the key of C first.

Use this basic rhythm:

Fig. 20.3. Rhythms for "12-Bar Blues 3"

Then, transpose to G, D, A, E, F, B♭, and E♭.

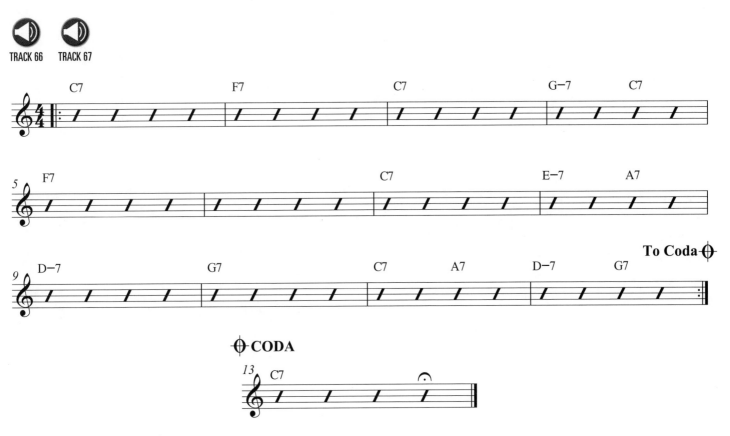

Fig. 20.4. 12-Bar Jazz Blues

LESSON 21

Practicing with Rhythm Tracks, CDs, Sequences, and the Metronome

Many sequencers, such as Logic and Garage Band, allow you to create a sequence of a rhythm section, which is an excellent tool to practice comping. Some keyboards have built-in rhythm tracks and features that allow you to record your playing and listen to it. Recording your playing and then listening analytically is one of the best ways to improve your comping and soloing. Write down your observations. If you don't like what you hear, why don't you like it? How can you change it? If you like what you hear, why do you like it? Can you reproduce it again in other keys? Transcribe your comping.

Practicing with recordings where the keyboard track is silent, such as those that come with this book, is also valuable. You can also play along with famous jazz groups on recordings and try to copy the keyboard player's comping.

The metronome is a useful tool for comping. Practice comping on beats 2 and 4 in swing time, with the clicks on 2 and 4.

Building Repertoire

Building repertoire and transposing aren't just comping topics, of course: it has to do with all aspects of being a musician, even if you are not going to be a performer. Obviously, if you plan to be a working musician, you need to have a large repertoire of standards (or other styles of tunes), and the only way to develop that is to set goals for yourself for learning tunes. All jazz piano players should have a working knowledge of several hundred jazz standards as their goal, which includes playing the melody. The way repertoire and transposition relate to comping is this: If you know the chord progression of a tune, you can transpose it into any key. Then, if you are in a situation in which you are the accompanist to a vocalist who does not have a chart transposed into his or her vocal key, you will have no trouble comping in that key.

When I got my first solo piano gig, I set the goal of learning two new tunes a week. Before long, I was up to over a hundred tunes memorized. (I now have a repertoire of over a thousand tunes.) It's a good idea to learn a new tune in all twelve keys. Transposition skill is particularly valuable when you are comping for a singer. Even if you can just comp on the chord changes, you will become a better composer, arranger, or sound engineer.

PRACTICING TRANSPOSITION

To develop your transposition skills, start with 12-bar blues (see lesson 20), and practice in all twelve keys. Then, listen to track 68, and practice figure 22.1 in all twelve keys. Then, practice comping with track 69 (no keyboards), and transpose into all twelve keys.

TRACK 68   TRACK 69

B♭ Rhythm Changes

Fig. 22.1. B♭ Rhythm Changes. Comp using LH only, then both hands.

Discography: Listening to Examples of Great Comping

Brubeck, Dave. "In Your Own Sweet Way." *Workin' with the Miles Davis Quintet.* The Miles Davis Quintet. Prestige 7166, 1959.

Davis, Miles. "Blues by Five." *Cookin' with the Miles Davis Quintet.* The Miles Davis Quintet. Prestige 7094, 1957.

Davis, Miles. "Four." *Workin' with the Miles Davis Quintet.* The Miles Davis Quintet. Prestige 7166, 1959. Red Garland, piano. You will notice how spare the comping is but that each chord is intentional and means something in the rhythmic punctuation. He comps for Miles Davis and John Coltrane on this early Miles CD (1956). Other good tracks from this CD are "In Your Own Sweet Way" and "Half Nelson." Also check out Red on "Blues by Five" on Miles' *Cookin' with the Miles Davis Quintet.*

Davis, Miles. "Half Nelson." *Workin' with the Miles Davis Quintet.* The Miles Davis Quintet. Prestige 7166, 1959.

Davis, Miles. "Someday My Prince Will Come." *Someday My Prince Will Come.* The Miles Davis Sextet. Columbia CS-8456, 1961. Wynton Kelly, piano. Deceptively simple sounding and very beautiful (lead sheet is in *The Real Book,* only be warned, the changes are not correct!).

de Paul, Gene. "You Don't Know What Love Is." *Saxophone Colossus.* Sonny Rollins, Tommy Flanagan, Doug Watkins, Max Roach. Prestige 7079, 1956.

Hancock, Herbie. "Cantaloupe Island." *Empyrean Isles.* Herbie Hancock, Freddie Hubbard, Ron Carter, Tony Williams. Blue Note ST-84175, 1964.

Hubbard, Freddie. "Red Clay." *Red Clay.* Freddie Hubbard. CTI 6001, 1970. Herbie Hancock, piano. Herbie is playing Fender Rhodes piano. Notice the rhythm hits in the melody. The lead sheet is in *The Real Book.* You don't have to listen to the entire 12-minute track to get the idea.

Mancini, Henry. "The Days of Wine and Roses." *Affinity.* Bill Evans. Warner Bros BSK 3293-Y, 1978. Bill Evans, piano. Listen to how he comps for Toots Thielmans (harmonica player), Larry Schneider on tenor sax, and for himself when he is taking a solo.

Rollins, Sonny. "Blue 7." *Saxophone Colossus.* Sonny Rollins, Tommy Flanagan, Doug Watkins, Max Roach. Prestige 7079, 1956. Tommy Flanagan, piano. Top comping picks are "You Don't Know What Love Is" and "Blue 7."

Werner, Kenny. "Chess Mates." *Tones Shapes & Colors.* The Joe Lovano Quartet. Soul Note 121132-2, 1986.

Glossary

"A" and "B" position voicings	four-way close rootless voicings with tension substitutions
anti-groove	accenting beats 1 and 3, which prevents forward motion
close position	chord voicing with chord tones and tensions in small intervals (major 3rd or less)
Dorian mode	the mode built on the second degree of the major scale using only notes diatonic to that scale; very common in jazz
groove	basic rhythmic pulse achieved in swing time by accenting beats 2 and 4
inversion	one of two positions besides root in a triad, one of three positions besides root in a seventh chord
lay out	hipster's term for not comping
open position	chord voicing with or without roots containing intervals larger than a fourth (also called "spread")
rhythm changes	a series of chord changes, 32 bars, based on the chords in the Gershwin song "I Got Rhythm," commonly played in jazz with many different melodies
spread	see "open position"
tension	upward extension of a seventh chord
tension substitutions	replacing a chord tone with a tension, such as 9 substitutes for R, or 13 for 5
voicing	an arrangement of chord tones and tensions in which tensions often substitute for chord tones

About the Author

Photo by Jennifer Williams

Jazz pianist and composer Suzanne Davis is active internationally as a performer, leading her jazz trio and quartet regularly in Boston, New York City, and Paris. An alumna of Wellesley College, she is associate professor of piano at Berklee College of Music. She has composed music for several films, including *In Between* directed by filmmaker and actress Deborah Twiss. Recordings include *The Suzanne Davis Quartet: First Set, Hymn to Freedom,* and *A High Tolerance for the Truth.* Her original composition, *Transition Waltz* was featured in a short animated film and received *Print* magazine's 1999 Digital 6 Award. She has performed with Joe Hunt, Ted Kotick, Herb Pomeroy, Greg Hopkins, Phil Grenadier, George Garzone, and Grover Washington Jr. Recordings and videos of her music can be found on suzjazz.com.

"An outstanding talent"
—Ernie Santosuosso, *The Boston Globe*

"A wonderfully talented pianist. [Her playing is] sensitively hued and deftly intuitive."
—Ron della Chiesa, *WGBH Radio*

"She tackles a group of chestnuts by such composers as Gershwin, Cole Porter, and Rodgers and Hammerstein, managing to make them sound fresh and new."
—Bob McCollough, *The Boston Globe*

More Fine Publications

Berklee Press

GUITAR

BEBOP GUITAR SOLOS
by Michael Kaplan
00121703 Book $16.99

BLUES GUITAR TECHNIQUE
by Michael Williams
50449623 Book/Online Audio..........$24.99

BERKLEE GUITAR CHORD DICTIONARY
by Rick Peckham
50449546 Jazz – Book..........................$12.99
50449596 Rock – Book..........................$12.99

BERKLEE GUITAR STYLE STUDIES
by Jim Kelly
00200377 Book/Online Media $24.99

CLASSICAL TECHNIQUE FOR THE MODERN GUITARIST
by Kim Perlak
00148781 Book/Online Audio..............$19.99

CONTEMPORARY JAZZ GUITAR SOLOS
by Michael Kaplan
00143596 ....$16.99

CREATIVE CHORDAL HARMONY FOR GUITAR
by Mick Goodrick and Tim Miller
50449613 Book/Online Audio..............$19.99

FUNK/R&B GUITAR
by Thaddeus Hogarth
50449569 Book/Online Audio $19.99

GUITAR CHOP SHOP – BUILDING ROCK/METAL TECHNIQUE
by Joe Stump
50449601 Book/Online Audio $19.99

GUITAR SWEEP PICKING
by Joe Stump
00151223 Book/Online Audio..............$19.99

INTRODUCTION TO JAZZ GUITAR
by Jane Miller
00125041 Book/Online Audio $19.99

JAZZ GUITAR FRETBOARD NAVIGATION
by Mark White
00154107 Book/Online Audio $19.99

JAZZ SWING GUITAR
by Jon Wheatley
00139935 Book/Online Audio..............$19.99

A MODERN METHOD FOR GUITAR*
by William Leavitt
Volume 1: Beginner
00137387 Book/Online Video $24.99
*Other volumes, media options, and supporting songbooks available.

A MODERN METHOD FOR GUITAR SCALES
by Larry Baione
00199318 Book............................$9.99

Berklee Press publications feature material developed at the Berklee College of Music.
To browse the complete Berklee Press Catalog, go to
www.berkleepress.com

BASS

BASS LINES
Fingerstyle Funk
by Joe Santerre
50449542 Book/CD $19.95
Metal
by David Marvuglio
00122465 Book/Online Audio.............$19.99
Rock
by Joe Santerre
50449478 Book/CD $19.95

BERKLEE JAZZ BASS
by Rich Appleman, Whit Browne, and Bruce Gertz
50449636 Book/Online Audio $19.99

FUNK BASS FILLS
by Anthony Vitti
50449608 Book/CD $19.99

INSTANT BASS
by Danny Morris
50449502 Book/CD $9.99

VOICE

BELTING
by Jeannie Gagné
00124984 Book/Online Media $19.99

THE CONTEMPORARY SINGER – 2ND ED.
by Anne Peckham
50449595 Book/Online Audio $24.99

JAZZ VOCAL IMPROVISATION
by Mili Bermejo
00159290 Book/Online Audio $19.99

TIPS FOR SINGERS
by Carolyn Wilkins
50449557 Book/CD $19.95

VOCAL TECHNIQUE
featuring Anne Peckham
50448038 DVD...........................$19.95

VOCAL WORKOUTS FOR THE CONTEMPORARY SINGER
by Anne Peckham
50448044 Book/Online Audio..........$24.99

YOUR SINGING VOICE
by Jeannie Gagné
50449619 Book/Online Audio $29.99

WOODWINDS/BRASS

TRUMPET SOUND EFFECTS
by Craig Pederson & Ueli Dörig
00121626 Book/Online Audio..............$14.99

SAXOPHONE SOUND EFFECTS
by Ueli Dörig
50449628 Book/Online Audio $15.99

THE TECHNIQUE OF THE FLUTE: CHORD STUDIES, RHYTHM STUDIES
by Joseph Viola
00214012 Book...........................$19.99

PIANO/KEYBOARD

BERKLEE JAZZ KEYBOARD HARMONY
by Suzanna Sifter
00138874 Book/Online Audio...........$24.99

BERKLEE JAZZ PIANO
by Ray Santisi
50448047 Book/Online Audio $19.99

BERKLEE JAZZ STANDARDS FOR SOLO PIANO
Arranged by Robert Christopherson, Hey Rim Jeon, Ross Ramsay, Tim Ray
00160482 Book/Online Audio...........$19.99

CHORD-SCALE IMPROVISATION FOR KEYBOARD
by Ross Ramsay
50449597 Book/CD.......................$19.99

CONTEMPORARY PIANO TECHNIQUE
by Stephany Tiernan
50449545 Book/DVD $29.99

HAMMOND ORGAN COMPLETE
by Dave Limina
50449479 Book/CD $24.99

JAZZ PIANO COMPING
by Suzanne Davis
50449614 Book/Online Audio $19.99

LATIN JAZZ PIANO IMPROVISATION
by Rebecca Cline
50449649 Book/Online Audio...........$24.99

SOLO JAZZ PIANO – 2ND ED.
by Neil Olmstead
50449641 Book/Online Audio...........$39.99

DRUMS

BEGINNING DJEMBE
by Michael Markus & Joe Galeota
00148210 Book/Online Video $16.99

BERKLEE JAZZ DRUMS
by Casey Scheuerell
50449612 Book/Online Audio............$19.99

DRUM SET WARM-UPS
by Rod Morgenstein
50449465 Book..........................$12.99

A MANUAL FOR THE MODERN DRUMMER
by Alan Dawson & Don DeMichael
50449560 Book..........................$14.99

MASTERING THE ART OF BRUSHES – 2ND EDITION
by Jon Hazilla
50449459 Book/Online Audio...........$19.99

PHRASING: ADVANCED RUDIMENTS FOR CREATIVE DRUMMING
by Russ Gold
00120209 Book/Online Media...........$19.99

WORLD JAZZ DRUMMING
by Mark Walker
50449568 Book/CD $22.99

STRINGS/ROOTS MUSIC

BERKLEE HARP
Chords, Styles, and Improvisation for Pedal and Lever Harp
by Felice Pomeranz
00144263 Book/Online Audio $19.99

BEYOND BLUEGRASS
Beyond Bluegrass Banjo
by Dave Hollander and Matt Glaser
50449610 Book/CD $19.99

Beyond Bluegrass Mandolin
by John McGann and Matt Glaser
50449609 Book/CD $19.99

Bluegrass Fiddle and Beyond
by Matt Glaser
50449602 Book/CD $19.99

EXPLORING CLASSICAL MANDOLIN
by August Watters
00125040 Book/Online Media $19.99

THE IRISH CELLO BOOK
by Liz Davis Maxfield
50449652 Book/Online Audio $24.99

JAZZ UKULELE
by Abe Lagrimas, Jr.
00121624 Book/Online Audio $19.99

BERKLEE PRACTICE METHOD

GET YOUR BAND TOGETHER
With additional volumes for other instruments, plus a teacher's guide.
Bass
by Rich Appleman, John Repucci and the Berklee Faculty
50449427 Book/CD $16.99

Drum Set
by Ron Savage, Casey Scheuerell and the Berklee Faculty
50449429 Book/CD $14.95

Guitar
by Larry Baione and the Berklee Faculty
50449426 Book/CD $16.99

Keyboard
by Russell Hoffmann, Paul Schmeling and the Berklee Faculty
50449428 Book/Online Audio $14.99

WELLNESS

MANAGE YOUR STRESS AND PAIN THROUGH MUSIC
by Dr. Suzanne B. Hanser and Dr. Susan E. Mandel
50449592 Book/CD $29.99

MUSICIAN'S YOGA
by Mia Olson
50449587 Book $17.99

THE NEW MUSIC THERAPIST'S HANDBOOK – 2ND EDITION
by Dr. Suzanne B. Hanser
50449424 Book................................... $29.95

AUTOBIOGRAPHY

LEARNING TO LISTEN: THE JAZZ JOURNEY OF GARY BURTON
by Gary Burton
00117798 Book $27.99

HAL•LEONARD®

Prices subject to change without notice. Visit your local music dealer or bookstore, or go to **www.berkleepress.com**

MUSIC THEORY/EAR TRAINING/ IMPROVISATION

BEGINNING EAR TRAINING
by Gilson Schachnik
50449548 Book/Online Audio $16.99

THE BERKLEE BOOK OF JAZZ HARMONY
by Joe Mulholland & Tom Hojnacki
00113755 Book/Online Audio........... $27.50

BERKLEE MUSIC THEORY – 2ND ED.
by Paul Schmeling
Rhythm, Scales Intervals
50449615 Book/Online Audio $24.99
Harmony
50449616 Book/Online Audio $22.99

IMPROVISATION FOR CLASSICAL MUSICIANS
by Eugene Friesen with Wendy M. Friesen
50449637 Book/CD $24.99

REHARMONIZATION TECHNIQUES
by Randy Felts
50449496 Book $29.95

MUSIC BUSINESS

ENGAGING THE CONCERT AUDIENCE
by David Wallace
00244532 Book/Online Media.......... $16.99

HOW TO GET A JOB IN THE MUSIC INDUSTRY – 3RD EDITION
by Keith Hatschek with Breanne Beseda
00130699 Book..................................... $27.99

MAKING MUSIC MAKE MONEY
by Eric Beall
50448009 Book $26.95

MUSIC LAW IN THE DIGITAL AGE – 2ND EDITION
by Allen Bargfrede
00148196 Book..................................... $19.99

MUSIC MARKETING
by Mike King
50449588 Book.................................... $24.99

PROJECT MANAGEMENT FOR MUSICIANS
by Jonathan Feist
50449659 Book.................................... $27.99

THE SELF-PROMOTING MUSICIAN – 3RD EDITION
by Peter Spellman
00119607 Book.................................... $24.99

MUSIC PRODUCTION & ENGINEERING

AUDIO MASTERING
by Jonathan Wyner
50449581 Book/CD............................ $29.99

AUDIO POST PRODUCTION
by Mark Cross
50449627 Book $19.99

THE SINGER-SONGWRITER'S GUIDE TO RECORDING IN THE HOME STUDIO
by Shane Adams
00148211 Book/Online Audio............. $16.99

UNDERSTANDING AUDIO – 2ND EDITION
by Daniel M. Thompson
00148197 Book..................................... $24.99

SONGWRITING, COMPOSING, ARRANGING

ARRANGING FOR HORNS
by Jerry Gates
00121625 Book/Online Audio........... $19.99

BEGINNING SONGWRITING
by Andrea Stolpe with Jan Stolpe
00138503 Book/Online Audio $19.99

BERKLEE CONTEMPORARY MUSIC NOTATION
by Jonathan Feist
00202547 Book................................... $16.99

COMPLETE GUIDE TO FILM SCORING – 2ND ED.
by Richard Davis
50449607 .... $29.99

CONTEMPORARY COUNTERPOINT: THEORY & APPLICATION
by Beth Denisch
00147050 Book/Online Audio......... $22.99

THE CRAFT OF SONGWRITING
by Scarlet Keys
00159283 Book/Online Audio........... $19.99

JAZZ COMPOSITION
by Ted Pease
50448000 Book/Online Audio $39.99

MELODY IN SONGWRITING
by Jack Perricone
50449419 Book..................................... $24.99

MODERN JAZZ VOICINGS
by Ted Pease and Ken Pullig
50449485 Book/Online Audio $24.99

MUSIC COMPOSITION FOR FILM AND TELEVISION
by Lalo Schifrin
50449604 Book $34.99

MUSIC NOTATION
PREPARING SCORES AND PARTS
by Matthew Nicholl and Richard Grudzinski
50449540 Book.................................... $16.99

MUSIC NOTATION
THEORY AND TECHNIQUE FOR MUSIC NOTATION
by Mark McGrain
50449399 Book.................................... $24.95

POPULAR LYRIC WRITING
by Andrea Stolpe
50449553 Book $15.99

SONGWRITING: ESSENTIAL GUIDE
Lyric and Form Structure
by Pat Pattison
50481582 Book.................................... $16.99
Rhyming
by Pat Pattison
00124366 2nd Ed. Book $17.99

SONGWRITING IN PRACTICE
by Mark Simos
00244545 Book.................................... $16.99

SONGWRITING STRATEGIES
by Mark Simos
50449621 Book.................................... $22.99

THE SONGWRITER'S WORKSHOP
Harmony
by Jimmy Kachulis
50449519 Book/Online Audio $29.99
Melody
by Jimmy Kachulis
50449518 Book/Online Audio $24.99